A Bird Watcher's Guide to
BLUE JAYS

By
Katherine Ponka

 Gareth Stevens
PUBLISHING

Please visit our website, www.garethstevens.com. For a free color catalog of all our high-quality books, call toll free 1-800-542-2595 or fax 1-877-542-2596.

Library of Congress Cataloging-in-Publication Data

Ponka, Katherine, author.
 A bird watcher's guide to blue jays / Katherine Ponka.
     pages cm. — (Backyard bird watchers)
 Includes bibliographical references and index.
 ISBN 978-1-4824-3836-9 (pbk.)
 ISBN 978-1-4824-3837-6 (6 pack)
 ISBN 978-1-4824-3838-3 (library binding)
 1. Blue jay—Juvenile literature. 2. Bird watching—Juvenile literature. I. Title.
 QL696.P2367P66 2016
 598.8'64—dc23
                                    2015018164

First Edition

Published in 2016 by
Gareth Stevens Publishing
111 East 14th Street, Suite 349
New York, NY 10003

Copyright © 2016 Gareth Stevens Publishing

Designer: Laura Bowen
Editor: Therese Shea

Photo credits: Cover, pp. 1 (blue jay), 7 Tom Reichner/Shutterstock.com; cover, pp. 1–32 (paper texture) javarman/ Shutterstock.com; cover, pp. 1–32 (footprints) pio3/Shutterstock.com; pp. 4–29 (note paper) totallyPic.com/ Shutterstock.com; pp. 4–29 (photo frame, tape) mtkang/Shutterstock.com; p. 4 (robin) Martha Marks/Shutterstock.com; p. 4 (blue jay) MVPhoto/Shutterstock.com; p. 4 (crow) Evgeniia Litovchenko/Shutterstock.com; p. 5 Don Johnston/ All Canada Photos/Getty Images; p. 6 iKandy/Shutterstock.com; p. 9 Shooty Photography/Shutterstock.com; p. 11 Bruce MacQueen/Shutterstock.com; p. 12 (eggs) Jeffthequiet/Wikimedia Commons; p. 12 (baby birds) Photo Researchers/Science Source/Getty Images; p. 13 (main) Zimiri/Shutterstock.com; p. 13 (inset) Ram-Man/ Wikimedia Commons; p. 15 rck_953/Shutterstock.com; p. 17 (main) Nancy Rose/Moment Open/Getty Images; p. 17 (inset) Nancy Bauer/Shutterstock.com; p. 19 (both) Danita Delimont/Gallo Images/Getty Images; pp. 21, 26 Sylvie Corriveau/Shutterstock.com; p. 22 Nick Saunders/All Canada Photos/Getty Images; p. 23 Redwood/ Shutterstock.com; p. 25 Merydolla/Shutterstock.com; p. 27 Jackie Smithson/Shutterstock.com; p. 28 Joel Sartore/ National Geographic/Getty Images; p. 29 Donald Gargano/Shutterstock.com.

Printed in the United States of America

CPSIA compliance information: Batch #CW16GS: For further information contact Gareth Stevens, New York, New York at 1-800-542-2595.

CONTENTS

Words in the glossary appear in **bold** type the first time they are used in the text.

NOISY NEIGHBORS!

robin

blue jay

crow

It was the "jay! jay! jay!" call of the blue jay that made me want to be a bird watcher. When I heard that noise, I looked around, and there was a pretty blue bird. I wanted to know more about it. So, I started this journal to write down what I see and learn.

The blue jays in my yard like to sit in the trees and talk. They're bigger than robins, but not as big as crows. I read that they're part of the **corvid** family of birds.

Blue jays are easy to spot because of their bright blue color.

BRIGHT BLUE JAYS

BLUE JAY COLORS

shades of blue, black, and white above

white or light gray underneath

I found a few blue jay feathers on the lawn this morning. The feathers aren't actually blue. Do you want to know something weird? The feathers only look blue because of the way light hits them. The **pigment** in blue jay feathers is actually brown.

I love watching the little **crest** of feathers on a blue jay's head. I can tell how it's feeling. When it's happy and calm, the crest is flat. But when it's excited, mad, or afraid, the crest stands up high.

This blue jay
must be excited!

HOW OLD?

Measuring Up

about 11 inches
(28 cm) long

weigh about
3 ounces
(85 g)

wingspan of
about 16 inches
(41 cm)

I'm watching a blue jay on a branch right now. I wonder how old it is? I know blue jays usually live to be about 7 years old. One **banded** blue jay lived more than 17 years. Wow!

Now, another blue jay lands next to the one I'm watching. I wonder if they're a pair? Blue jays often **mate** for life. They lay eggs each year between March and July. But first they have to build a nest!

Male and female blue jays have the same coloring and are the same size.

NEST KNOWLEDGE

Bird-Watching Tip!

Blue jays will leave the nest for a few hours if they feel unsafe. That's why I'm using my binoculars. I don't want to scare them!

I saw a blue jay building a nest in the outer branch of a tall tree. The tree is between my yard and my neighbor's yard. My neighbor told me blue jays like to build nests 10 to 25 feet (3 to 7.6 m) off the ground.

Looking through my **binoculars**, I could see that the nest was shaped like a cup made out of twigs. I read that the male brings most of the supplies. The female builds the nest just how she likes it!

RAISING A FAMILY

blue jay clutch = 2 to 7 eggs!

I've been watching the mother blue jay sit on her nest. I read her eggs are called a clutch. I also read that her eggs are blue or light brown with brown spots.

I'm going to watch this nest every day. In about 17 days, I'll see little heads pop up. Then, in about 3 weeks, the young blue jays will try to fly for the first time! I can't believe how fast they grow!

Baby blue jays don't look much like their parents at first. They soon grow their colorful feathers.

13

DEFENDERS OF THE NEST

Copy . . . Bird?

You've heard of a copycat? A blue jay can copy other animals' sounds. One even learned to sound like a cat!

Just like I thought, the eggs have **hatched**! I've been busy watching the parents feed the babies. They'll feed their babies for up to 2 months after they learn to fly.

Today, I learned that blue jays **defend** their babies! There was a hawk in the yard, looking at the nest. The parents chased it away. Hawks, owls, and falcons may eat blue jays, so it was brave of the parents to do that. Babies are also hunted by squirrels, cats, snakes, crows, and raccoons.

Baby blue jays may leave the nest before they learn to fly. The parents won't feed them unless they return to the nest.

FEEDING BLUE JAYS

What They Eat

- peanuts
- seeds
- fruits
- grains
- acorns
- bugs
- small birds
- eggs
- caterpillars

Blue jays are fun to feed because they like so many different foods. Two of their favorites are acorns and peanuts. I once saw a blue jay put five whole peanuts in his throat and beak! Blue jays also eat nuts, seeds, fruits, and grains. They may bury acorns and seeds in the ground for later. This is called a cache.

My bird book said that blue jays sometimes eat other birds' eggs and babies. Yuck! I think I'll feed them more peanuts!

Blue jays like open flat feeders that don't move.

17

BATHING BLUE JAYS

SUET RECIPE

I put some homemade **suet** treats near the birdbath. Here's how I made them:

2 cups peanut butter
2 cups lard
½ cup each of flour, rolled oats, peanuts, raisins, sunflower seeds, and chopped corn

Melt peanut butter and lard. Mix all ingredients in a large pan and cool until hardened. Cut into squares.

I read that blue jays really like birdbaths. I decided to use the money I got for my birthday to buy one. There were lots of different kinds at the store. I chose one that was wide and deep. There's room for a whole blue jay family to splash around.

We put the birdbath near the window, so I can watch the birds from inside the house. The blue jays found it today! They cleaned themselves, but also drank from the bath.

Some birdbaths are heated so they don't freeze in winter.

19

STAY OR GO?

The Blue Jays' Range

North America

This shows where blue jays can be found.

Last winter, I fed lots of birds. Blue jays' bright blue colors were easy to spot in the snow. Sometimes they fly south for the winter, and sometimes they don't. Some **migrate** one year, but not the next! Scientists don't know why.

The ones who do fly south travel in big groups high in the sky. They may fly in groups of over 200! I would love to see so many bright blue birds all at once.

Young blue jays are more likely to migrate. But adults may, too.

21

BLUE JAY BEHAVIORS

The blue jays in my yard make me laugh when they swoop down and scare the squirrels. I saw one sit near the feeder and heard it make a sound like a hawk: "Kee-eeeee-arr!" The other birds flew away, and the blue jay ate the food alone!

In my bird book, I learned that blue jays molt, or lose their feathers, each year. They then catch ants and rub them on their skin! Scientists think something in the ants' bodies makes the birds' skin feel better or may clean their skin.

Blue jays aren't afraid of guarding their food!

23

HOMEMADE HOUSE

MY PLANS

8"

10"

12'

I want to build a birdhouse for the blue jays. I know they like an open **platform**. I asked my dad for help. He'll have to use a ladder to attach the house to a tree since they like to nest up high.

I plan to put a roof on the house, so the birds have shade and won't get wet. They'll be able to hide from predators, too. If a blue jay pair likes it, they'll come back year after year. I hope so!

Fall and winter are the best time to set up a new birdhouse.

HOMEMADE FEEDER

I made my own bird feeder, too. Mom helped me put big holes in a log. I filled them with suet and peanut butter. I hung the feeder from a tree branch near the birdbath, but close to the window. That way, I'll be able to spot the birds when I'm inside the house!

Keeping blue jays safe is an important job for a bird watcher. I put the feeder close to trees and **shrubs**, so the jays can easily hide if they don't feel safe.

Other birds like my log bird feeder, too! This is a red-breasted nuthatch.

My Log Feeder

KEEPING THEM CLOSE

REMINDER :

Join a bird-watching group! Check out: www.audubon.org

Did you know blue jays are gardeners? When they bury seeds and nuts, they sometimes forget to come back and get them. These then grow into trees and plants. So, helping blue jays is like helping nature!

I make sure to keep my feeder and birdbath clean so my blue jays stay healthy. If I do my part, I can watch beautiful blue jays all year. When they sing and swoop around my yard, I know I'm a good backyard bird watcher!

When blue jays don't have a feeder nearby, they eat what nature provides!

29

GLOSSARY

banded: fitted with a band for tracking and identification, usually for research purposes

binoculars: handheld lenses that make objects seem closer

corvid: a bird of the family that includes crows, jays, and magpies

crest: a growth of feathers on the head of a bird

defend: to protect somebody or something from attack, harm, or danger

hatch: to come out of an egg

mate: to form a couple for the purpose of raising babies

migrate: to move to warmer or colder places for a season

pigment: a substance that gives plant or animal matter color

platform: a raised structure with a flat surface

shrub: a low, woody plant with many stems

suet: a type of hard fat found in animals, sometimes used to make food for birds

FOR MORE INFORMATION

Books

Berendt, John. *My Baby Blue Jays.* New York, NY: Viking Press, 2011.

Mara, Wil. *Blue Jays.* New York, NY: Cavendish Square Publishing, 2015.

Websites

Blue Jay
www.biokids.umich.edu/critters/cyanocitta_cristata
This is a fun site to learn more about blue jays.

Blue Jay—A Beautiful Backyard Bird
www.grandpas-backyard-fun.com/blue-jay.html
Check out this great resource for blue jay information.

Create a Certified Wildlife Habitat
www.nwf.org/How-to-Help/Garden-for-Wildlife/Create-a-Habitat.aspx?
Learn how to make your backyard a place birds want to be.

Publisher's note to educators and parents: Our editors have carefully reviewed these websites to ensure that they are suitable for students. Many websites change frequently, however, and we cannot guarantee that a site's future contents will continue to meet our high standards of quality and educational value. Be advised that students should be closely supervised whenever they access the Internet.

INDEX